# Taking Charge
## My Reaction Almost Cost Me Everything

# Taking Charge
## My Reaction Almost Cost Me Everything

**by**

# Tramanica Jackson Watson

# Acknowledgement

I would like to dedicate *Taking Charge* to my incredible husband Dionell (but I call him "My Watson"). He always encourages me to be comfortable with who I am. My three beautiful daughters; Helene, Chelsea, and Taylor, that tell me they are proud that I am their mother. To my mother Helen, who has never left my side throughout this journey. My auntie Linder, in my darkest times, you would always have an encouraging word. I would like to thank my family and friends for being patient with me as I figured out this thing called life. To all the great women and men of God that has poured into my life, I praise God for your wisdom. Most importantly to my Lord and Savior Jesus Christ for giving me another chance.

# Take Charge Moments


Introduction.........................................1

The Day I Died........................5

How Did I Get Here?....................10

The Thief Called Regret..............15

Cost of Denial.........................18

When the Dust Settled................21

The Haunting..........................25

Everyone Has a Turn...................30

The Cave..............................34

Imaginary Dilemma....................37

Be Careful…………………………..40

Identity Crisis……...………………..43

Facing the Giants……...….…….……47

The Awakening……...……………..50

# **Introduction**

**Luke 22: 31,32(NIV)**

31 And the Lord said, Simon, Simon, behold, Satan hath desired *to have* you, that he may sift *you* as wheat:

32 But I have prayed for thee, that thy faith fails not: and when thou art converted, strengthen thy brethren (sisters).

Life has a sense of humor, ha-ha!! Right when you think you have it all together, here comes trouble. It walks down the street with a narcissistic smirk on its face waiting to see whose life it can turn upside down. We all know on this side of heaven life comes in all aspects, not always good or bad. We must remember never to discount the bad days because it will make you appreciate the good. The word says life is like a vapor slowly fading away. So, why sit around waiting for things to get better. We must take the bull by the horn and not look back. Because no matter how much you plan, some things are unavoidable. It only takes one phone call to shatter your world to pieces. All you can do is work with what you have left and make the best out of it. Mama said a hard head makes a soft…Well you know the rest.

Discounting wisdom, ignoring signs, and wasting time feeling I was entitled to respect, I learned that no matter how hard you try, there will always be critics shooting subliminal bullets hoping to finally hit its target and get you to abandon your assignment. I can talk about it because there was a season, I left my post. Waiting around for the applause or the cosign that says, "You got it, Sis!" Throughout the book, you will find out that it did not happen, and I had to take charge of my life. People will tell you not to worry about who left you instead of celebrating the ones who stayed. That is easier said than done when you have invested so much and one day it's all gone. I was telling everyone else to release it and let it go, and I was still holding on for dear life. But on the inside, I was like a ticking time bomb waiting to go off, "BOOM!!!" I had my fight with Regret, and it won. Things that I should have buried, I keep resuscitating. Forgetting the good but replaying the bad repeatedly, like picking the skin off a wound that almost healed. Believing today will be a better day just to wake up to the same issue.   The demons I didn't want to face. Now, I am not here to point the finger or blame anyone for the trials and tests I had to endure. Instead, I say thank you because it made me the woman I am today. No longer a victim but walking in VICTORY, evaluating the past, preparing for the future, and not rushing today.

This is my story, "Taking Charge,"…My reaction almost cost me everything.

# The Day I Died

As I lay in the bed enjoying my day off from work, I suddenly heard a knock on the door. My oldest daughter said, "Mama, can you take Ethan to daycare"? The expression on my face said no, but I knew that was not an option. As I was getting up out of the bed I began to think, "Can I get one day for me?"

Oh yes, I love the little fellow, but today I did not want to be grandma. All I wanted to do was rest. After dropping my grandson off, a heaviness came over me as if something were about to happen. I prayed Lord give me the strength to endure any heartache that may occur. My mind began wondering about all the things that I needed to be doing.  Suddenly out of nowhere, I went on an emotional rollercoaster. The tears started to roll uncontrollably, and I began beating on the steering wheel, screaming to my inner self, "Why me?" I didn't recognize this person that was crying out from within me.  That person was confused and full of resentment. "Who is there?" I thought. The response I got was from Anger. You have ignored me for the past three years.  You know the last years had been full of hurt, judgment, sickness, loss, abandonment, and betrayal, but you pretended I did not exist, masking me with smiles and keeping busy. Saying, "You are strong; you do not need anybody. It is their loss. God removed them because they are not going into my future." At that moment, I tried to out talk Anger and began defending myself. I have done all I was supposed to do. I feed the elderly. I did outreach in the community. Each year we sacrifice and gave a single mother's shoes for school and coats for Christmas for her kids. I gave my last, and I gave up my old life. I felt like I was on an emotional rollercoaster as I switched again, saying, "Lord forgive me. If I need to ask someone for forgiveness, whatever I need to do, please take this pain away." At that moment, I felt like I had stop breathing and died. No funeral, no flowers, no ashes to ashes, dust to dust, no one gave their last words. I did not even have a headstone that says, "Here lays

Tramanica Jackson Watson." That day I felt like a failure to others but mainly myself. I thought I would be further in life. I felt like I had wasted a lot of time doing things that were not a part of my destiny—thinking how I went through an eleven-month storm. From stroke, to laid off, to thyroid problems to tumors in the breast—I survived. I had been knocked down so many times and still managed to get back up. But this time, it was different. My name had been assassinated by the people that once said they loved me. I was devastated and broken before the Lord. See, the truth is, I found out I was not relying on God. I depended on my abilities to fix things. Yes, me in my limited power. And most of the time, I just made a mess of it. I had not let go of my anthem        "I-N-D-E-P-E-N-D-E-N-T. Thank God he is merciful and kind. He was waiting for me to surrender. Once I acknowledged that I needed the Lord, I knew that I needed to get out those ashes and walk in my beauty. As time went on, I realized this was part of my elevation process, and I failed miserably. I prayed to the Lord, "Give me another chance. I am not ready to die. People are counting on me to succeed because when I win, they win." My family needed me to live. They required me to be whole. At that moment, it was as if I heard the paramedics say, "We're losing her." All of a sudden, the Lord breathed restoration in me. I could fill the air coming back into my body and a still, small voice that said, "Now, breathe."

# Now let's go back before that day…

# How Did I Get Here?

Growing up in the Baptist church, I learned so many lessons from integrity to obedience. I started teaching Sunday School at age fifteen. Those little sunbeams, as they were called in the early '80s, were a joy. But my proudest moment was when I was sixteen years old; I became president of the Jr. choir. That day was our anniversary, and my name was in bold print **"Tramanica Jackson, President."** As the double doors of the church opened, everyone stood. The choir marched in singing, "We're Marching Up to Zion." I took the lead in my royal blue dress that Derrick had made for me. I can hear him now saying, "Girl, they were hating, you killed it." I was smiling throughout the service, sitting with my legs slightly crossed by the ankle. This was the first day I felt important. As I look at it now, it was a foreshadowing of the person I would be—the "First Lady." After the service, everyone was giving me compliments about how beautiful and organized everything was. Then I heard a small voice that said, "This is only the beginning." Years passed, and everything seemed to be on track, even though I strayed a little. Now, I'm married to a wonderful man. We have three beautiful, young ladies plus a handsome grandson. By this time, my husband and I started our first storefront ministry, "Connected 2 the Kingdom." Life could not be any better. Then one day, a terrifying thing happened. I realized I was in a place that I had not prepared. Trial after trial, from losses to betrayal, abandonment, and death, it seemed like a bad dream for eighteen months that would not end.

At first, I was in denial and held my emotions. Battling from within, I began to talk to myself. I am strong, a daughter of the Kingdom, the pastor's wife. They say give; I gave. They said love; I loved, even the ones that talked about me behind my back. I barely had time for myself, always willing to help others.

The truth was I was going around the same circle, hoping to get different results, exhausted in mind and body, being pulled in every direction. I had not figured out how to just say NO! The saying goes, if you handle God's business, he will take care of yours. Honestly, God did not require me to do half the things I was doing. When it is God, he will give you grace for the assignment. I went from having Saturday morning women's prayer meetings and a Monday night women's fellowship to nothing. One day I was surrounded by women to the next day on my knees, just God and me. Never would I dream of having past due bills, unemployment, repossessions, divorce, betrayal, or abandonment being a part of my resume. Thinking I should be further than this, why me? What did I do to deserve this pain? Nobody told me how hard this would be. Life had hit me so hard that I felt like the wind was knocked out my body. I was lifeless and numb, not including embarrassed and ashamed to the point I checked out of society. The rumor was we had moved to Mississippi. Never I could imagine being given the cold shoulder from some of the same people that sat at my table. This was a part of my new reality, and I had to deal with it. It did not happen overnight, but one day I woke up and knew I could not keep focusing on how I got here, but how I get out.

**Take Charge Moment**: Never get so comfortable in your position that you feel it cannot happen to you.

# The Thief Called Regret

So much happened in a short time. I lost my car; my ministry took a hit, and some "friends" walked away. In the end, I almost lost my mind. It had been five months since the worst storm of my life; I was ready to pick up the pieces and rebuild. Little did I know I did not resolve some critical issues. Blinded by my drive to move on, Regret sabotaged my new place of peace. The foundation built on "what if's" and the roof constructed of "I should haves". My walls cemented fear. No need for windows because the world had built this house around me and left me for dead. I did not need a door because I did not want anyone to come in.

We think we are protecting ourselves from the outside, but we have closed out the people that love us. It was so overwhelming at times that I would sit in the dark and cry myself to sleep. I missed so much time with my family that I could have enjoyed. Because I did not confront Regret, it opened other emotions that became overwhelming. My regrets turned into depression. It had taken over my life. Depression is sneaky; it does not knock on your door and say I am here. It gradually infiltrates your life and takes over your mind, heart, and soul. Don't be deceived a lot of people function depressed. I found myself not caring about anything, not even myself. What difference does it make if I'm a well-dressed failure?  I let my family down; most importantly, I let God down.

Regret stole my passion and took

control of my life. It was like I had the angel of light on one shoulder telling me to get up God has a plan. And the angel of darkness on the other telling me to give up. "Nobody loves you; it's not worth it. Walk away and leave it all behind; nobody will miss you." Funny thing is, I knew the word of God, but most days, the enemy won.

**Take Charge Moment**: Never did I think of suicide. That is a sensitive matter in my family. I could not bear knowing hurting the people I loved.

# Cost of Denial

When hurt and pain make a reoccurrence in our life, denial can become our identity—always pumping life back into a dead-end relationship, never wanting to let go and hoping that it was just a little misunderstanding. I did not want to accept they said what they said and showed me who they were. I wanted to be wrong about specific people, but the betrayal was staring me in my face. I lost respect and it was a long way back to trust. What I should have done was walk away and disconnect but the feeling of being an outsider was hard to swallow. What I learned is you cannot be friends with the friend that dishonored you.

Eventually, a decision must be made, them or you. I put myself through unnecessary turmoil because I did not want to accept the truth. All I had to do was move on and let them go. We all want validation, a feeling of acceptance, if it's honest or not. So many people have ulterior motives that sometimes it is hard to discern. Many times, we want to see what we want to see, knowing its far from the truth. My husband always says, "You must know where to place people in your life." Everyone cannot handle who you are, so you only open the door to let certain people come in. It is ok not to have a plus one everywhere you go. It is better to admit that there are seasons of separation that you must walk through. Stop denying the truth. It will save you from a bunch of heartaches.

**Take Charge Moment**: Denying something happened does not take away the act it did. Denial is depriving yourself of the truth in front of you.

# When the Dust Settled

Looks can sometimes be deceiving. Have you ever been to a circus and seen the trick of a dove appearing out of thin air? One minute the magician has fire in his hand, and as he blows it out, a dove appears. That trick is easy because the fire was on special paper, and the dove is in a secret compartment made in the sleeve of the jacket the magician is wearing. The magician puts the fire out by waving the paper; that's when he opens the secret compartment, and shazam, a dove appears. There are people just like the magic trick. They show you one thing, but their identity is hidden, waiting for the right moment to be revealed. I had met several people who tricked me into thinking they were all about the Watsons when they had their own agenda. Certain parts of my journey, the Lord has not permitted me to speak on, so I must be mindful. There's an old saying my grandma use to tell; "What does not come out in the wash, it will come out in the rinse." This incident made me see what she meant, and it shook my soul. My husband and I had a thriving ministry on television ministering in a different place, and then one day, the enemy visited us without making an appointment. He disguised himself as a brother, and because we had let our guard down, we didn't recognize he was a wolf in sheep's clothing. As time passed, an uprise in the church came upon us. Like Jesus, some of the same people who were responsible for our success were also behind our demise. That's another story for another time. In the end, people left and giving declined. We tried our best to keep the place, but the rent was $3,300 a month, not including all the other expenses. Eventually, the owner offered us a smaller place, but we didn't have extra money to remodel another building. It took over $10,000 to renovate the building we had. So, the owner put a for sale sign on the building. As I drove up that Sunday morning, I sat in my car, trying to get myself together. How am I going to face the few people we have left?  As I looked up, I heard a couple laughing and whispering, "That's what they get." My heart almost stopped with hurt, and tears ran down my face with disbelief. I couldn't believe what I was hearing. After all, we had been through; this was like a slap in the face. To this day, I never revealed to them that I know how they felt.

**Take Charge Moment**: Never let them see you sweat.

# **The Haunting**

When I was a teenager, those were some of my fondest memories. At age fifteen, I got my first car. It was a blue two-door Maverick. Those were the good old days, going to football games, hanging out with the crew in the parking lot of Winn Dixie grocery store, and house parties. One thing I did not like about being a teen was puberty. This process is when your body evolves from a child to a young adult. Everyone has a different experience and mines was acne. It took over my body with black dots on my back, arms, and face. I tried every kind of cream and face wash and nothing seemed to work. So, I just endured the criticism. Don't all teenagers go through this? To make this long story short, this boy liked me, and I did not like him. He was annoying and I just wanted to be a teenager. I did not want a boyfriend hanging around me everywhere I went. Well, one day, I missed school. The next day I came back, a girl in my class came to me with tears in her eyes saying, "I didn't know!" "You didn't know what?" I asked. He told everyone in the class that I had skin cancer to shame me. When that did not work, he started calling me a chocolate chip face. That nickname spread like wildfire. I had lost confidence and I began to look at myself as if I was the ugly duckling. That was the first time I battled with negative words, but it would not be my last. As years passed, my self-esteem was damaged. I let my standards down to accepting any man and any friend.

You can hear, "You're ugly", and

"You're fat and nobody wants you" so much that your self-image is ripped in pieces. It begins to take root in your life. Just like a tree, what you see on top of the ground is not the whole tree. The roots are deep underneath. You can say I was like a tree—confident on the outside, but underneath my roots, insecure. It is like you're held hostage in a cage without a lock on the door. The saying, "Words will never hurt" is not true because it can paralyze you for the rest of your life. It's like a disease that eats away at you from the inside out, not seen by man's eyes, only through the soul. I had to develop a thick skin over the years because I would have aborted God's assignment for me if I did not. There were some that I considered as friends, but when I lost it all treated me like a peasant. They just tolerated me, giving me flowers I thought were real but found out they were plastic. The hardest part about the experience is the treatment of the church folks. You go to church for healing but instead, I got abused. In many settings, I was prejudged before I even arrived. I understand why the man on the street corner passes by and don't want to come into the church building. When they decide to come, many sit in the corner with their arms folded, whispering instead of greeting them with the love of Christ. This is a misrepresentation of who Jesus is. Where is the love and compassion in the body of Christ? I will never forget speaking at a women's conference, and afterward, a lady came up to me and said, "You're nothing like what they say." Wow! What a way to start a conversation, but at least she was honest.

In the midst of all the negativity in my life, I met my husband.  The past pain that I had not let go almost destroyed us even before we began. He was loving and always giving me words of affirmation.  He would say things like, "Hello beautiful", "Girl, you fine", and "I love you." Even after years of marriage, because of the unbreakable influences of my past, I could not receive his compliments. I'm getting better now, but just like other things, it's one day at a time.

**Take Charge Moment**: Let go of the past words someone else that was not even worth your time spoke about you.

# Everyone Has a Turn

My youngest daughter, as a child, loved playing dress-up in my clothes. Anything from scarves, hats, and belts, she would pull out my closet and pretend she was a model. When she would try to walk in my high heels, her little ankles shook as she pretended to walk on the runway. She would say, "Look mama, I can almost wear them." She can finally wear my shoes physically, but it does not mean she can handle the reality of what came with them. We must remain silent on things that we cannot comprehend. The word says, "Don't judge unless we want to be considered" [Matthew 7:1 (NIV)]. I dare not speak on something that I have not walked through because everyone has a turn. Everyone sees the reaction but does not know the cause. There are a lot of people that love to play the victim after they have caused the chaos. As time passed, I have learned that every action does not demand a reaction. Even when you know you're right, there is a time to speak and a time for silence. Many times, we feel we must defend ourselves. That part of me had to die. How can you just let someone get away with a lie? I must defend it, not knowing it will make it worse. I had to get away from the noise and seek God. "Vengeance is mines saith the Lord, I will repay" [Romans 12: 19 (NIV)]. Wow! That sounds good, huh? But what happens when it is you? They lied and made you look bad when all you did was help them. Look at it this way, God sees all and knows all, and if you trust him, you will come out victorious. I will never forget I tried to help a young lady, but instead, she turned on me and claimed I said some unbelievable things. Oh! That is why I am receiving stares and rolling of the eyes! It took my breath away, feeling suffocated by the words. For years I would see her on social media and feel hurt. One minute I was like Naomi (sweet), then my disposition changed to Mara (bitterness). You see, when you have given your all and invested in something and it turns on you it will cause a shift in your life. Gradually, you begin to lose yourself and become someone you never thought you would. Sadly, you cannot see it, but everyone around you feels the effects. We have a certain time to mourn over some issues in life. If we do not mourn properly, we will begin to set up bitterness. I could not figure out why, even after I prayed and fasted, there was no flow. It was as if I hit a roadblock in my ministry and had to sit and wait until everything cleared. I heard the spirit of the Lord say to me, "Once you stop being bitter, I will open your womb again." That was a hard pill to swallow.

**Take Charge Moment**: Do not alter your integrity during adversity. While you're waiting on God's vengeance you will miss out on your Victory.

# The Cave

When some people come out of significant suffering, they crawl in their hole and make-believe world, hoping to block out everything and everybody. I felt that it was better if I block the noise out and isolate myself, it will all just disappear. Not only did it influence others, but I didn't realize it had trickled over to not caring about myself. I felt like a loser and began to accept where I was in life as if it was all my fault. I played the isolation game and went inside a make-believe cave. That cave was like being stuck in an elevator and not being able to breathe. Hearing the echo of my struggles screaming back at me, "God look what they did to me!' I was an emotional wreck, and I was taking everything personal. My discernment was off, and I felt attacked on every side. I was clapping back even before there was a clap back. I needed to defend myself like being summoned to the Supreme Court. What I love about God is that he didn't let me stay in that cave too long without chastising me. It was like God said, "Stop that whining and complaining." He reminded me of 2004. I took sick, went from 152 to 118lbs. I had suffered two light strokes, surgery for fibroids, and problems with my thyroids where at times, I could only get a whisper out all within eleven months. I will never forget when I put on some white capri pants and a baby blue shirt. I went to a Revival service, and the man of God said it was never about you; it was always for them. At that time, it did not make sense, but now I get it! My struggles, setbacks and challenges were all part of my resume and my testimony. At that moment, my thinking began to change. I needed that cave for a season to see myself and what I had become.

**Take Charge Moment**: The negative perception others have of you should never influence your thought pattern.

# Imaginary Dilemma

Everyone has their likes and dislikes, and there is no explanation. My daughter doesn't like cheese but loves pizza. I love the beach but don't enjoy getting in the water. The mind can be extremely complicated. What you think is simple, I may feel it as significant. It is all about perception. Experiences will take you from the glass half full to half empty. When you have gone through so much, you can become mentally exhausted trying to find that place of peace. My thinking had become cloudy, thinking everyone was against me. Even some of the most remarkable things that were said about me I always felt, "Who sent you?

What is your motive? What do you want?" The struggles and things you have overcome will put you in a place where you must always defend yourself. Why am I saying this? Because if you do not recognize you need help, it will take you to a place of hopelessness. We came to this world alone and will leave it alone, so why would you want to live independently? The old church mother would say, "If I got Jesus, I do not need anybody else." That sounds good, but it is not the truth. The scripture says the Lord told Adam, "It's not good for you to be alone" [Genesis 2:18 (NIV)]. We all need someone to talk to, love, to share our lives with. So, I had to stop blocking people who God sent and wanted to see the best come out of me.

**Take Charge Moment:** Everyone is not out to see you fail, and if you think this way, you will miss out on who God has sent to help you.

# Be Careful

Many times, wise counsel is rejected because it is not easy to face the truth. It's not on purpose, but pain has a way of speaking so loudly, it can block out the good for the bad. How can my vision be so cloudy that I've missed this, but I can see that? Everyone's story is different. Some have been abandoned by the person that promised to love them. The person that says, "I do," even the one that gave birth to them. The person that you gave your last to and trusted with your inner thoughts and secrets can be that same person who will betray you at your lowest. How do you handle it? There was a time in my life I needed someone to lean on. I was in rehab for emotions and was almost on my last step. I thought I found the right person to help me with the latter part of that journey. They had been hurt in some of the same ways I had been. They were so sensitive to my feelings. I was relieved that I had someone to vent to without judgment. That made me more and more comfortable to open myself up to them. As time passed, they took the mask off. Everything I shared was used against me to sabotage my name. She labeled me as crazy and disrespectful. I should have listened to my Auntie Linder, when she warned me to pay close attention to what people say and how they say it. I get it now Auntie! Crazy is one thing I'm not, but I learned to just be careful. If you call protecting myself from going back into that dark place of pain and hurt disrespectful, that's fine also. I'll disconnect from every outlet before I go back to that place. I had lived many years under the radar disguised as a ministry.

**Take Charge Moment**: Now, I am careful who I vent to because when you rise above them, they will use your failures as a weapon.

# Identity Crisis

If you do not know who you are, people will give you a title and an assignment that God disapproves of. Some people reveal one word of knowledge, and now the people are labeling them a prophet. That is where the battle began because we all have the grace to run the race the Lord has set before us. Thank God I am comfortable with who the Lord has made me to be, a Teacher. Honestly, it took time for me to figure out who I was and not mimic the YouTube evangelist that I admired so much. Once you find that place of purpose, do not let no devil in hell move you from that place—you are needed in the

Kingdom. Over twenty years ago, a Prophetess at the church said some people want to get close cause they want your life. I am thinking, "Lady, you are crazy. What do I have?" It didn't take long for the truth to come out. I'll never forget that a lady in the ministry brought another lady to the church saying she had a prophecy, but it was a rebuke. The first mistake was I did not take anyone with me to be a witness. The things she shared with a smile on her face were horrible.  It broke my spirit. Never would I have thought someone that came in the name of the Lord would say those awful things. The second mistake I made was I allowed her to get so close to me; I thought I could learn from her. Once I shared it with my husband, he reminded me it was only to bring a level of doubt, fear, and unbelief. It did not take long to find out she did not want to mentor me; she wanted to be me. I was just as anointed but walking in fear, and she knew it.

See, she had studied me and my eagerness, not knowing I was accepting crumbs from the table full of spoiled food and it was making me sick. Listen, everything that someone brings to you is not necessary for you to you receive it. We must declare the word of the Lord and not what the devil sends. Just because they are titled prophet or have thousands of followers, it does not mean its God. Maybe it has not manifest yet, but it doesn't mean God didn't' say it. Wake up, know who you are in God, and don't let an enemy tell you otherwise. You are who God says you are.

**Take Charge Moment:** Mentorship is essential for spiritual development.

# Facing the Giants

There are two things I learned throughout this journey:

**1. You must admit your hurt**. How can you heal if you do not acknowledge there is a problem? Yes, that hurt. Yes, I was mad, and yes, I quit. I deserved to be celebrated for the things I had done, and because that did not happen, I set in my sorrows with a pity party. I was consumed with binge watching *Lifetime* when I should have been building friendship and growing in the things of the Lord. Can I share something with you? If you have to cry, scream, or whatever you must do for your release, then do it. Do not dwell on it because an idle mind is the devil's workshop. He wants you to be in denial and play the blame game, so then he can get you to isolate yourself. That's when he can work on your mind and heart to get you away from the truth. Remember, the truth will set you free.

**2. Time of mourning.** It is ok to mourn but just do not stay there. Give the problem an expiration date. I heard a story about a man who gave himself five minutes a day to talk about his troubles, and that was it. Think about it. Is it worth it to continue to bring up who shot Johnny? At this point, it does not matter. You have cried and vented, now get up and let it go. Freedom is a choice, but it also requires action. I know you have seen the picture of a horse tied to a plastic chair. The horse has more power than the chair, but he doesn't know it. All he has to do is move. We are more significant than our adversary, with the help of the Lord, but we must renew our minds. Think about things that were good and not evil. Remind yourself of the promises of the Lord and how he sees you and not others. You are who God says you are. Even though you may have to weep for a season, joy is around the corner.

**Take Charge Moment**: In this life, trouble will not cease. In the words of Reinhold Niebuhr, "God, grant me the serenity to accept the things I cannot change, courage to change the things I can, and wisdom to know the difference."

# The Awakening

Sometimes we find ourselves exhausted and not sure which way to go. My smiles and laughter were no indications of my happiness, but it was a cover-up of hurt. Functioning like a zombie—not alive but going through the motions of day to day, bringing sounds of busyness to my life to drown out the sounds of fear. I was tired of pretending. I had fallen asleep, just like the disciples when Jesus asked them, "Can you watch for one hour?" It was time to wake up and take the mask off, remember the day I died. Once I surrendered, the Lord breathed life back unto my body. That is when Take Charge began.

I had to take my power back. In life,

you will always have critics. For too long, I allowed the insecurities of others to dictate how I have seen myself. Everything that happens doesn't require a reaction. I've learned silence is sometimes the best weapon. My steps have been ordered and I'm better for it. Never allow anyone to have the authority over your life and never look back. It is over and I am over it. The battle is not mine to fight; it is the Lords. I've learned that if people feel you win, they are your biggest cheerleader, but once you lose, only a few will stay. Now that I know who is really on my side, it makes things better. I am no longer bitter. Instead, I'd rather take the "L" now than keep investing years into someone that would abandon me at my lowest time. I found my place of peace, and now I can dream again. My focus is no longer on others' opinions, walking with my head down because I do not match their expectations. Now, I am living with confidence, knowing I am a daughter of the Kingdom.  Yes, I will make mistakes in the future, but they will not define me. I changed my position on the team. No longer on the side of the defense. I have awakened, and I got it!! My smile is not fake its real.  I take myself out to eat.  I am getting manicures and pedicures, celebrating me and taking the time to enjoy my family.  I am free to be me!

**The moral of the story is**: _"Take Charge"_ of your life. Why are you waiting?  Its time. Oh, you thought someone was going to cosign you and say, "Yes, sis!  You can do it"!

Sometimes, it is just you and God. Now ladies, Release, Regroup and Recover!


P.S., I almost forgot. We packed up and moved to Texas with the pieces we had left. Stay tuned!

www.ingramcontent.com/pod-product-compliance
Lightning Source LLC
Chambersburg PA
CBHW051009050726
47592CB00007B/2776